PRAI
The Psalm

MW01001208

"The Psalm on the Cross is an outpouring from a living reservoir deep within David Roseberry's heart. The book masterfully illuminates the reality that Jesus owned Psalm 22 as his own and prayed its opening words in a sorrowful but confident hope. This truth is beautifully expressed through the writer's pen. The book Invites the reader to dive deeply into the mystery of human suffering and rise with a joyful confidence of hope in and through Christ. I welcome this book for my private devotions, for use in small groups and parish-wide ministry, and as valuable gifts for friends no matter where they are on their spiritual journeys."

—Ron McRary, CANON FOR GROUP LIFE AT ALL SAINTS IN DALLAS, TX

"David Roseberry is the perfect guide to this psalm—and to meeting Jesus through it. This is the rare book I could give every single person in my church: it's deep for the longtime saints yet so clear and approachable that the people exploring faith for the first time will connect with it also."

—Kevin Miller, RECTOR OF CHURCH OF THE SAVIOR IN WHEATON, IL; CO-FOUNDER OF PREACHINGTODAY.COM

THE PSALM ON THE CROSS

A Journey to the Heart of Jesus through Psalm 22

BY DAVID H. ROSEBERRY

ANGLICAN COMPASS

AN IMPRINT OF LEADERWORKS
PROSPER, TEXAS

THE PSALM ON THE CROSS:
A Journey to the Heart of Jesus through Psalm 22
Copyright © 2021 by David H. Roseberry

Published by Anglican Compass, an imprint of LeaderWorks. Learn more at anglicancompass.com.

ISBN
Paperback 978-1-7358461-1-8
E-book 978-1-7358461-2-5

ANGLICAN COMPASS
AN IMPRINT OF LEADERWORKS
1080 FIREWHEEL LANE
PROSPER, TEXAS 75078

AnglicanCompass.com

Published in the United States of America

For Those who Love
our Lord and His Cross

Table of Contents

Acknowledgements

I AM GRATEFUL for so many blessings in my life, chief among them is my wife Fran. Her support and encouragement has been jet fuel for me for nearly four decades. She read a few chapters in the early formation of this book and encouraged me to keep going. She is wind in my sails. Thank you, love.

The people of Christ Church in Plano came to my mind often as I wrote this book. They were those who attended years and years of Good Friday liturgies and heard me read Psalm 22 out loud at those Holy Week services. I never did preach a sermon on Psalm 22 and so perhaps this book is a compilation of those I might have preached.

I am also thankful for those who read, reread, and improved this manuscript with their suggestions and comments. John Wallace, Amber Gallaway, Patty Woodmansee, Chick Schoen, Penna Dexter, John Tuthill, and Bruce Barbour. My new friend, David Jacobsen helped me with the final draft.

The people who offered their public endorsements have stuck their necks out, and I am thankful to them too. Erika, Paul, John, Ron, and Kevin—bless you. May the Lord reward you for your bravery!

The mysteries that I have tried to present and describe in this work are too big for words. I struggled to convey these ancient truths of our Lord's passion, death, and victory. If I failed in my attempts, it is the fault of the writer (me), not the Word.

Finally, it is probably expected that I would acknowledge and give thanks to God for His amazing love, but I want to express even more. The partnership that our God had with the writers of the Bible is one of the most mysterious miracles I can think of. How did God, through the inspiration of the Holy Spirit, work in an Israelite king to see something he would never experience and write poetry that would find its fulfillment 1000 years later in a descendant son of his own? It truly bogles my mind—but it fills my heart with faith and joy.

Epigraph

(THIS PSALM) MAY HAVE been actually repeated word by word by our Lord when hanging on the tree; it would be too bold to say that it was so, but even a casual reader may see that it might have been. It begins with, *"My God, my God, why hast thou forsaken me?"* and ends, according to some, in the original with *"It is finished."*

For plaintive expressions uprising from unutterable depths of woe we may say of this psalm, "there is none like it." It is the photograph of our Lord's saddest hours, the record of his dying words, the lachrymatory of his last tears, the memorial of his expiring joys.

Before us, we have a description both of the darkness and of the glory of the cross, the sufferings of Christ and the glory which shall follow. Oh, for grace to draw near and see this great sight! We should read reverently, putting off our shoes from off our feet, as Moses did at the burning bush, for if there be holy ground anywhere in Scripture it is in this psalm.

—Charles H. Spurgeon

Psalm 22

1 My God, my God, why have you forsaken me?
Why are you so far from saving me,
from the words of my groaning?
2 O my God, I cry by day, but you do not answer,
and by night, but I find no rest.

3 Yet you are holy, enthroned on the praises of Israel.
4 In you our fathers trusted; they trusted, and you delivered them.
5 To you they cried and were rescued;
in you they trusted and were not put to shame.

6 But I am a worm and not a man,
scorned by mankind and despised by the people.
7 All who see me mock me;
they make mouths at me; they wag their heads;
8 "He trusts in the LORD; let him deliver him;
let him rescue him, for he delights in him!"

9 Yet you are he who took me from the womb;
you made me trust you at my mother's breasts.
10 On you was I cast from my birth,
and from my mother's womb you have been my God.
11 Be not far from me, for trouble is near,
and there is none to help.

12 Many bulls encompass me; strong bulls of Bashan surround me;
13 they open wide their mouths at me,
like a ravening and roaring lion.
14 I am poured out like water,
and all my bones are out of joint; my heart is like wax;
it is melted within my breast;
15 my strength is dried up like a potsherd,
and my tongue sticks to my jaws; you lay me in the dust of death.
16 For dogs encompass me; a company of evildoers encircles me;
they have pierced my hands and feet—

17 I can count all my bones— they stare and gloat over me;
18 they divide my garments among them,
and for my clothing they cast lots.

19 But you, O LORD, do not be far off!
O you my help, come quickly to my aid!
20 Deliver my soul from the sword,
my precious life from the power of the dog!
21 Save me from the mouth of the lion!
You have rescued me from the horns of the wild oxen!

22 I will tell of your name to my brothers;
in the midst of the congregation I will praise you:
23 You who fear the LORD, praise him!
All you offspring of Jacob, glorify him,
and stand in awe of him, all you offspring of Israel!
24 For he has not despised or abhorredthe affliction of the afflicted,
and he has not hidden his face from him,
but has heard, when he cried to him.

25 From you comes my praise in the great congregation;
my vows I will perform before those who fear him.
26 The afflicted shall eat and be satisfied;
those who seek him shall praise the LORD!
May your hearts live forever!

27 All the ends of the earth shall remember
and turn to the LORD, and all the families of the nations
shall worship before you.
28 For kingship belongs to the LORD, and he rules over the nations.

29 All the prosperous of the earth eat and worship;
before him shall bow all who go down to the dust,
even the one who could not keep himself alive.
30 Posterity shall serve him;
it shall be told of the Lord to the coming generation;
31 they shall come and proclaim his righteousness to a
people yet unborn, that he has done it. (ESV)

Overview

"My God, my God, why have You forsaken Me?"

THESE WERE THE DYING WORDS OF JESUS as he hung on the Cross on Mount Calvary. But what did He mean by them?

Jesus's painful ordeal on the Cross began around 9 in the morning and ended at 3 p.m. During those six hours on the Cross, Jesus spoke only a few times. The Gospel records seven of these statements.[1] All of these last words of Jesus give extraordinary insights into His heart and His faith in His Father, and His love for all people.

One statement is found in both the Gospel of Matthew and Mark. In these two accounts, Jesus was heard to say, *"My God, my God, why have You forsaken Me?"*, which is the opening verse of Psalm 22. This supplication is both a lament and a pleading question. It is one of the most passionate and intense moments in all of Scripture—the Son of God praying the opening line of this 1,000-year-old psalm.

But what did Jesus mean by saying it? What does it tell us about Him that he quoted it?

This book is an in-depth look at Psalm 22, and it is framed by a single assumption. Namely, that Jesus meant more than just the opening verse. He had the *entire psalm* on His mind and in His heart. *"My God, my God, why have You forsaken Me?"* was the overture for everything else that is written in this psalm of suffering and, as we will see, in this psalm of victory.

All 31 verses of Psalm 22 contain the full intent of what Jesus meant when he spoke the first verse. The entire psalm represents the content of our Lord's heart.

After crying out the first line of the psalm, Jesus may have prayed the rest of it silently the way we pray a prayer from memory. He may have whispered the psalm under His labored breath. But in any case, Psalm 22 can help us see the progression of our Lord's thoughts. It is a reflection of our Lord's mind and heart. As we think through Psalm 22 line by line, we are able to think His thoughts and pray His prayers on the Cross.

Psalm 22 gives us an unparalleled opportunity to come close to Jesus's heart, to think about what He thought about on that lonely Cross, and to feel the depth of His emotion, commitment, and—in the end—His joy.

In this book, we will closely read Psalm 22 verse by verse, thought by thought. It will be like a pilgrimage. It will take us somewhere. Along the way, there will be signs, descriptions, and references to what was actually taking place on Mount Calvary where Jesus died. The psalm is very specific about what Jesus was enduring. As we walk through Psalm 22, we will gain surprising insights about what those final hours were like for our Lord. We will dwell on the deep thoughts that Jesus had during His ordeal. May we do this with great humility.

We know that King David wrote Psalm 22 ten centuries before the death of Jesus. Our Lord believed that David was not only a king, but a prophet. That is, Jesus thought that some of David's psalms were about His (Christ's) own life and work. He quoted from the psalms many times in His teaching and ministry. The Psalter (the collection of all 150 psalms) was Jesus's prayer book. He read them every day of His life. He studied them closely. Undoubtedly, He had them all memorized.

This guide will bring you to see the humiliation, the horror, and the triumph of our Lord's execution. Even though our Lord died in the full light of day, the psalm He prays will bring us into the dark night of His passion and death. The psalm will show us His love for His Father, even as His trust, faith, convictions, and confidence are tested and tried.

I hope this journey will be spiritually enlightening for you. I trust that you will find yourself loving God more because of our journey through Psalm 22.

If this book is being used as a Lenten reading program,

these chapters can be read day by day, beginning on Ash Wednesday and continuing each weekday until Friday before Palm Sunday. This book can also be used by any believer as a guide for mediation and prayer, especially on Good Friday or Holy Saturday. But as we experience Psalm 22, we must remember that when we stand near the Cross of Christ, we are standing on holy ground.

A final word: Do not leave yourself out of this story. After each of the chapters, I will encourage you to ask a few questions about what you have read and to think about what it might mean for your own life and walk of faith. As you will see, when we read Psalm 22, we discover that the entire Gospel is there. Therefore, I encourage every reader to see themselves as a humble recipient of God's unfailing love and to recognize the supreme gift that He has given us in the life, work, death, and resurrection of our Lord Jesus.

In Christ,
David H. Roseberry

I

Why?

My God, my God, why have you forsaken me?
Why are you so far from saving me,
from the words of my groaning? (vs. 1)

———————————

WHEN THE STORY OF JESUS'S CRUCIFIXION is told in the Gospel, Jesus is said to have spoken these words in Aramaic: *"Eloi, Eloi, lama sabachthani."*[2] Perhaps because these words are the most famous of Psalm 22, their depth nearly overshadows the rest of the 31 verses. These words, first written by King David 1,000 years earlier, begin one of the most passionate pieces of Hebrew poetry in the Bible. Jesus, like other rabbis, knew the Book of Psalms by heart, and He would have prayed or recited this particular one many times in His life.

We are told in the Gospel of Mark that when Jesus uttered these words, people in the crowd didn't understand Him. They thought He was calling on Elijah, perhaps because Eloi and Elijah are similar in sound.

Whatever the reason, it didn't matter, because He wasn't talking to them.

Rather, He was speaking to the God He knew, to the God He believed in, in His own language, Aramaic. He cried out to the God who had been His constant source of strength all of His earthly life.

From the beginning of the Gospel story about Jesus, His Father in Heaven had been a rock of assurance; a steady constant in His life. Once, in His early years, while returning from an annual family trek to Jerusalem, Jesus stayed behind.[3] His parents found Him teaching the Torah. When they asked Him why He had disappeared, His reply was simple: *"Didn't you know that I would be about my Father's business?"* This, at age twelve!

In His early thirties, after He was baptized, a voice from heaven confirmed His relationship to the Father. *"This is my Son in whom I am well pleased."* He said later that He and the Father were one. The bond between Father and Son was firm and fixed.

Jesus was very public about His unity relationship with His Father. When a massive crowd gathered for Hanukkah, He boldly proclaimed, *"I and the Father are One."*[4]

Yet on the Cross he asked, "Why?" Jesus felt forsaken and asked, "Why?"

Do not imagine that Jesus had lost His faith. This may be the thinking of modern scholars; that Jesus hung as a defeated doubter, a derelict in despair, a man with a

Marriages/Divorce; Leaving New Cal;
when ppl suffer under spiritual abuse

) Fine line btwn groanings too deep for words
or silence

1. "Why, God?" Remember a time when you asked this question before God. Jesus felt abandoned but He never stopped believing. Has this ever been true of you?

2. "A dead faith sounds like silence." What do you think of this comment?

3. The psalm is telling us that we can and should keep asking in our own prayers. What prayer of yours comes to mind when you read this?

II

Prayer

My God, my God, why have you forsaken me?
Why are you so far from saving me,
from the words of my groaning? (vs. 1)
O my God, I cry by day, but you do not answer,
and by night, but I find no rest. (vs. 2)
Yet you are holy, enthroned on the praises of Israel. (vs. 3)

———

WE SOMETIMES WONDER if God is deaf to our cries. Like Jesus on His Cross, we know that God is real, but for whatever reason, sometimes it seems that He does not hear us. Did Jesus think this way? It is a perfectly human thing to do. In this verse, Jesus cries out to God by day, but it says, *"…you do not answer."* While we know this feeling well, it is a new thing for our Lord to experience.

All of His earthly life, Jesus lived in daily, two-way communication with the Father. Jesus could be found in the morning, praying in a place so distant that the disciples would have to search to find Him. What was He doing there? He was praying. The Father's hand guided Jesus each day. In the evening, Jesus slept the sleep of one who was always near to the heart of God.

This is how Jesus could perform miracles; He displayed the power of God because He was thoroughly connected *with* the God of power. In the Gospel of Mark, there are a number of back-to-back stories that display the awesome power of Jesus.[5] Once, He spoke to calm a storm, and the wind and the waves were stilled. Another time, He spoke to exorcise a man from lifelong oppression by demons. Jesus spoke to the demons only once and they fled. He radiated such power and strength from His being that a sickly woman, on her own, approached Him just to touch His robe and be healed. Another time, he prayed over a girl and she was raised to life. Wherever He went and whatever He did, Jesus and the Father were One.

Put another way, *there is not a single instance of Jesus praying without receiving a clear and active response to His prayer.* Whatever He prayed for, that is what occurred. Every time.

But now, on the Cross, it is different. The psalm is not expressing doubt, but distance. Is the Father far away? There are many paradoxes in the psalm. This is one. The Father is both near and far. Surely, He listens, but it seems that He is deaf. These tensions are common in our walk of faith. But, as I say, Jesus is experiencing them for the first time.

This is why we discover dread in the second verse. Jesus says that He prayed, He cried out in the daytime, and for the first time ever, it seems that the Father did not hear. As most of us have, Jesus felt the fruitlessness of prayer. After years of close and confident connection, where was God?

Yet, even in the face of the silence from God, Jesus will not be silent Himself. He kept praying forward into what must have felt like a dark space, the empty place left behind after the Father seemingly had turned His face away. Still, He kept praying.

Years earlier, Jesus taught His disciples a parable to underscore the virtue of persistent prayer. At the end of His teaching, the disciples were all but commanded to pray constantly and to never give up. And now, on the Cross, Jesus is obedient to His own command. He prays this prayer.

Jesus would have been tempted to feel the despair of his dereliction. But even then, when there seemed to be no One listening, He prayed.

This can be one of the ways that we use psalms today. When we say a psalm, we find ourselves actually praying it, praying the written prayer of another. As Jesus did on the Cross, we can let the praying words of another become the words that we pray to our Father.

Did you know that the only thing the disciples asked Jesus to teach them was to pray? *"Lord, teach us to pray..."* they asked.[6] And here, on the Cross, Jesus is obedient to the lesson He taught. He prayed, even when it seemed that His prayers drifted into sounds of silence, the open and empty air. Let us pray.

CONSIDER AND COMMENT:

1. Who taught you to pray?

2. What do you pray for persistently?

3. When have you simply stopped praying for something because it seemed hopeless?

4. What happened?

faith; they are a deeply embedded, rock-solid trust.

A word that encapsulates the sense of this surprise is one of the most underused but powerful words in the life of faith: "nevertheless." Jesus says that though He feels the despair of being ignored by His Father in heaven, *nevertheless,* He knows that God is holy. Even though the prayers and cries of this perfect dying man seem unheard and unanswered, *nevertheless,* the God of Israel is holy.

Sometimes, if we choose to make a list of our lingering grievances, problems, and sorrows, we can grow weary and depressed. In this broken and fallen world, many things don't go right or don't go our way. There is ample room for worry and doubt every day. But the use of the word "nevertheless" can change the direction of our laments. This word means that we acknowledge the hard things around us, but yet we still choose to trust. "Nevertheless" is a word that takes us from being forlorn to being faithful.

When Jesus acknowledges the holiness of God, He uses a unique metaphor to show how God comes to people in distress and danger. Jesus says that God is the one who *"is enthroned on the praises of Israel."*

This phrase is found nowhere else in the Bible, and yet we sense exactly what it means. In times of great hardship and suffering, if we turn to worship, praise, singing, and deep expressions of thanksgiving, God seems palpably present to us. In this way, God inhabits our praise and worship.

Do you want to sense the presence of God in your life even in difficult or painful times? Tell God of your pain and suffering in prayers and petitions. Be real. Be honest. And then, as you conclude your prayer, add words such as these: "Nevertheless, I will trust and praise You, O God."

You will see that God inhabits your praise of Him.

Consider and Comment:

1. When have you prayed and felt that God responded with silence?

2. How does our praise and worship of God impact our faith in God?

3. How would you use the word "Nevertheless" in your personal prayers?

V

Memory

Yet you are holy, enthroned on the praises of Israel. (vs. 3)
In you our fathers trusted;
they trusted, and you delivered them.
To you they cried and were rescued;
in you they trusted and were not put to shame. (vs. 4–5)
But I am a worm and not a man,
scorned by mankind and despised by the people. (vs. 6)

WE JUST SAW HOW THESE VERSES SHOW US
the Savior's decision to trust God. But there is a good
reason for Jesus's trust and confidence in His Father.
Biblical history.

How did Jesus know the history of the ancient Israelites
and their relationship with God? The answer is simple: He knew the Scriptures. The texts, the teaching,
and the truths of the Israelites' history with God were
part of His daily life, weekly worship, and annual pil-
grimages to Jerusalem. He was formed by His ancient
faith. Jesus was steeped in the Scriptures. He knew God
could be trusted because His people had trusted Him
for thousands of years.

All of His life, Jesus was taught to read, remember, and recite the stories of the past. During His ministry, Jesus pulled quotes from the Hebrew Scriptures (our Old Testament) dozens of times, defining who He was and what He had come to do. There are 27 direct quotations from the Old Testament in the Gospel of Mark, 24 in Luke, and 14 in John's Gospel. In Chapters 11–16 of Mark, there are no fewer than 160 quotes or allusions to the Old Testament.[9] Matthew's Gospel contains all of Mark's quotations and adds another 30!

In other words, we cannot truly understand our role and calling as followers of Jesus without having some grasp on the content of the Old Testament.

The writers of the New Testament understood this. All told, there are 283 direct quotes from the Old Testament contained in the New Testament. The first Christians could not have imagined their faith without a clear grounding in the Scriptures of the Old Testament. Sadly, today, we often seem content to live with biblical amnesia.

We have forgotten our past. As we have lost our connection to sacred history, we have also lost our confidence in God. Worse yet, we forget that we have forgotten.

The entire Bible holds the key to our Christian identity because it shows us the overarching plan of salvation and how Jesus is the most significant figure in it.

Reading the whole of Scripture reminds us that we are a part of a people who can share evidence and give testimony to the responsiveness of God. To read and meditate on the Scriptures every day is to remind our inner soul and spirit of who we are and where we come from. Daily excursions into the pages of the Bible show us the amazing faithfulness of God over the years. Even now, as we "slow walk" ourselves verse by verse through the text of Psalm 22, Scripture teaches and reminds us to trust in a faithful God.

Why? Because faith is grounded in memory. If someone says they believe in God, but they have no working bank of memories of His Word or His actions from the past, they do not have faith. They have only a wish. *Hmmm...* They have only an unfounded hope for the future because they have no memory of the past.

Put simply, the key to a vibrant faith is a biblical memory. The most powerful tool that people have in their minds to live by faith is the ability to remember. Remembering God's faithfulness in the past will strengthen faith for what is ahead. Every time. When we pray our way through the many ways that God has been faithful in the past, we can better trust Him as we face our own unknowns.

The way we can rely on God for our future is based on how we remember the past.

Charles Spurgeon, the famous 19th-century Baptist

preacher, offers this aphorism to express this point: *"Out of sight out of mind; and out of mind, out of motive."*[10] He means that if we forget our past by placing it out of our mind, we lose our motive to walk forward.

We need to go back for our future.

CONSIDER AND COMMENT:

1. How important is our memory for a sincere personal faith?

2. On a scale of 1 to 10, how much of a grasp do you have on the timeline, events, and content of the Old Testament?

3. Restate Spurgeon's comment in your own words. What does it mean?

VI

Scorned

In you our fathers trusted;
they trusted, and you delivered them.
To you they cried and were rescued;
in you they trusted and were not put to shame. (vs. 4–5)
But I am a worm and not a man,
scorned by mankind and despised by the people. (vs. 6)
All who see me mock me;
they make mouths at me; they wag their heads;
"He trusts in the LORD; let him deliver him;
let him rescue him, for he delights in him!" (vs. 7–8)

UP TO THIS POINT, JESUS'S PRAYER has been theological. As He has embodied the words of doubt, longing, and faith in the psalm, we have been able to stand somewhat apart from the events on Calvary and observe. The next few verses, however, take us into the terror of the moment.

Here, in verse six, the psalm changes perspective. Its focus is on the plaintiff. As Jesus recites the psalm verse by verse, it takes on a very personal meaning. Humbly, and with great sorrow and compassion, we are able to see into the heart of our Lord. When He remembers

39

the phrase, *"But I am a worm, and no man…"* He is speaking for the first time of Himself.

In the Book of Exodus, when our God first revealed Himself to Moses, He used a code phrase that is found in other places in the Bible. Do you remember the story? Moses was told by God to speak to Pharaoh and order the release of God's people from Egypt. Moses was reluctant. He wanted to have some answers to questions that the Israelites were sure to ask. Moses asked God, *"Who should I say sent me (to you)?"* God's answer is mysterious: *"Tell them, 'I AM sent you.'"* [11] This is God's name: I AM.

Simple? Hardly. There is more depth packed into those two words than we will ever fathom. "I AM" is the eternally present tense. God not only is the "I was," but He is also the "I will be" and the great "I am." He is the eternal now, who was and is and is to come. [12]

In the New Testament, the writer of John's Gospel exalts Jesus to the highest place in the universe. "In the beginning was the Word/Jesus, and the Word/Jesus was with God, and the Word/Jesus was God. He/Jesus was at the beginning with God. All things were made through him/Jesus, and without him/Jesus was not any thing made that was made." [13] And Jesus described Himself in exalted terms like this as well.

In John's Gospel again, Jesus used God's name from Exodus to speak of Himself. Seven times in the

VII

Worm

In you our fathers trusted;
they trusted, and you delivered them.
To you they cried and were rescued;
in you they trusted and were not put to shame. (vs. 4–5)
But I am a worm and not a man,
scorned by mankind and despised by the people. (vs. 6)
All who see me mock me;
they make mouths at me; they wag their heads;
"He trusts in the LORD; let him deliver him;
let him rescue him, for he delights in him!" (vs. 7–8)

OUR UNDERSTANDING OF THIS PSALM is building. We know that Jesus mentioned the first verse from the Cross, and we believe that Jesus intended the entire psalm to be His soliloquy, His final song. And as we read the lyrics to His last song, we can see into His heart, into what our Lord was feeling on the Cross.

In verse six, it is clear that Jesus associated Himself with the lowly worm. But even in this, we can see God revealing the great plan of salvation. Look deeply into the way the Bible tells us about this low form of life.

The Jewish rabbis have a teaching device that they use with their students. It is called *"remez."* The word means "hint," and it is similar to a hidden meaning. When a rabbi gives a remez, the student knows that there is more to a word or a verse than meets the eye.

Psalm 22:6 contains a remez.

Remarkably, the Hebrew word for worm, *"tola'at,"* is also the word for scarlet. The "tola worm" is scarlet or crimson because it is filled and colored with its own blood. In the ancient world, the Jews would harvest these grubs and crush them to obtain a dark crimson dye to color the fabric of the curtains in the Temple.

So, the image of the worm is not just about a tiny grub that means nothing to most people. Instead, this red worm points toward Christ. It is a *remez,* or hint, of the life of Jesus, and it contains a profound meaning when we ponder it. We can be certain that as Jesus was reciting and remembering Psalm 22 on the Cross, He knew specifically about the reference to the worm. And while he associates himself with it in its low, earthly form, He is also identifying Himself as the regal Son of God.

In fact, the ugly image of this fleshy grub is a beautiful image which, as we consider it, changes our perception of the verse. You see, when the female worm is ready to lay her eggs, which happens only once in her life, she climbs a tree or some other wood structure and attaches herself to it. Then a crimson shell forms a hard, protective covering under which the female deposits her eggs. The larvae hatch and feed off the blood and nutrients of the mother for about three days. Then as her life ends, she secretes a scarlet dye that stains the wood to which she is attached. The same dye colors her offspring; these baby worms remain scarlet or crimson for the rest of their lives.

But then something even more remarkable takes place. After three or four days, the tail of the mother pulls up into her head forming a heart-shaped body. The crimson color disappears, and it is replaced by a snow-white substance. It looks like a patch of wool on the tree before it flakes off and falls to the ground like snow.

The message could not be more obvious or wonderful: *"Come now, and let us reason together, saith the LORD: though your sins be as scarlet, they shall be as white as snow; though they be red like crimson, they shall be as wool."*[15]

CONSIDER AND COMMENT:

1. Have you ever felt as though God was using a passage of the Bible to give you a hint of something bigger? Explain.

2. Why would God reveal His plan of salvation in such a unique way?

3. Take a moment today to google the phrase "Crimson Worm." You will be amazed.

VIII

Blueprint

But I am a worm and not a man,
scorned by mankind and despised by the people. (vs. 6)
All who see me mock me;
they make mouths at me; they wag their heads;
"He trusts in the LORD; let him deliver him;
let him rescue him, for he delights in him!" (vs. 7–8)
Yet you are he who took me from the womb;
you made me trust you at my mother's breasts.
On you was I cast from my birth,
and from my mother's womb you have been my God. (vs. 9–10)

THESE WORDS SHOW US THE DEPTH of insult and scorn that Jesus endured. The text moves slowly through a dramatic progression of taunts. First, they laugh at Jesus. In the old King James Version of the psalm, it reads that they *"shoot out the lip,"* an expression that means to show off contorted faces and lash out with ugly insults. Then those who are gathered around the Cross shake their heads as if to say, "How pathetic…what a joke!" And then, most searing of all, the people take the words that Jesus had expressed earlier in verse 4—the words of hope and trust in God—and turn them against our Lord.

Do you see how the crowd is targeting not only the dying man on the Cross but the faith that upholds Him? Consider also that the mockers are not ill-advised or un-informed. As Matthew records Jesus's crucifixion, the people in the crowd taunting our Lord are not merely common folk. The instigators of this mean-spirited crowd are the chief priests and leaders of the religious establishment.

It is hard to believe that those who profess to know the most about God are the people most invested in the destruction of His Son.

It is hard not to let a terrible question enter our thinking about this dreadful scene at the Cross. It is a terrible question, and the answer might be terrible as well. Where would we be at the scene of this crime? Where would we stand? What would we say? Would we say anything at all? Would we be part of this ugly scene of ugly men yelling insults at our innocent Lord? God, I hope not. Please, God, I hope not.

As we are seeing in our slow walk through Psalm 22, all the verses are a roadmap or a blueprint of the events that took place at Golgotha 1,000 years after the psalm was written.

Interestingly, there is no known event in David's life that might have produced a text as deep, dark, and full of dread as Psalm 22. It is not a psalm describing the fate of a persecuted man (as some of the psalms are) or a man dealing with sickness or affliction (as many of the psalms do). Psalm 22 is a psalm about a gruesome execution, even though David lived 1,000 years before our Lord was crucified. How did this psalm ever come to be?

Some skeptics claim that Jesus or the Gospel writers took the events described in Psalm 22 and manufactured or reverse engineered the details of the crucifixion to fit it. They bent the events of Jesus's death to fit the details in the psalm. But this does not answer how the psalm came to be in the first place.

This question about the origin of Psalm 22 has an answer that will aggravate agnostics but bless believers. To my mind, the only possible answer is this: that the Holy Spirit inspired David to write about things he had never seen. The Spirit of God prompted him to describe an event that he had never attended. In the creative mind of King David, the Holy Spirit descended like the Muse and helped him imagine the most important event in all of history, ten centuries into the future.

David was Jesus's ancestor. They came from the same line and family tree. David did not know his Greater Son Jesus, but he did know what the Holy Spirit prompted him to write about Him. Amazing! It seems that every time we read the Bible closely and stay true to its content and context, it illuminates the life, teaching, death, and resurrection of Jesus Christ.

CONSIDER AND COMMENT:

1. Do the questions in the fourth paragraph trouble you?

2. Underline the phrase or sentence that stands out in this chapter. What do you notice about it?

3. How could religious leaders turn against Jesus? What were they afraid of?

IX

Mother

All who see me mock me;
they make mouths at me; they wag their heads;
"He trusts in the LORD; let him deliver him;
let him rescue him, for he delights in him!" (vs. 7–8)
Yet you are he who took me from the womb;
you made me trust you at my mother's breasts.
On you was I cast from my birth,
and from my mother's womb
you have been my God. (vs. 9–10)
Be not far from me, for trouble is near,
and there is none to help. (vs. 11)

WHAT WILL BE YOUR DYING THOUGHT?
Will your entire life flash before you? Will you remember only good times? Times of vacation? Work? Athletic victories? Intimate times? A wedding? What will you have as your final thoughts?

Here, just before his death, and in the face of a hostile crowd, the thoughts of our Lord go to His mother and to His birth. Jesus has in mind King David's words, but He has in His sight Mary, His mother. He might be looking at her. She is there. She is one of the few people who stayed with Him until the end.

Read verses 9 and 10 a few times to catch their meaning. In them, using the language of poetry, Jesus is praying the truth that God has been with Him from infancy. God the Father was the first to see Him enter the world; God is pictured as the midwife to Mary as she delivered her baby. And when Jesus is placed at her warm breast in a cold cave in Bethlehem, He had every hope in the world. *"...you were my hope..."*

Is there a more lovely or intimate scene in Jesus's life to imagine?[16] The Son of God was born a precarious baby into a human family in a remote corner of the Roman Empire. On the last day of Jesus's earthly life, He remembers the first day of His earthly life. He remembers His mother (who is standing near the foot of the Cross) and He remembers the delicate work of His Father as the midwife.

Something profound is stirring in these two verses. When we look at the two verses together, we see an indication of the miracle of the Incarnation. The psalm, as it would have been meant in Jesus's context, speaks about cooperation between God and Mary. Jesus is remembering His birth when the Lord God took Him (literally: "pulled me," Psalm 22:9) from the womb of Mary *and* also received Him from the womb. God is bringing forth Jesus and receiving Jesus as a newborn. Mary is a willing partner in this, to be sure. She offers the womb and the breast.

The tableau is beautiful. In this moment of suffering for our Lord, His mother is able to comfort Him by her steady presence at the Cross. She was there at the beginning of His life; she will be there at the end. This would have brought our Lord deep solace.

There are two doctrines of the Christian faith that are essential; they alone are the doctrines upon which everything else depends. First is the Doctrine of the Incarnation, whereby Jesus was born as a baby in a manger and was, at the same time, the Holy Child of God. And the second is the Doctrine of the Atonement that holds that Jesus's death on the Cross fundamentally altered our standing relationship with God. Because of Christ's death, we are now reconciled with God.

Remarkably, these two central beliefs are seen together on the Cross in the words of Psalm 22. In Psalm 22:9–10 on the Cross with His mother standing at His side, we behold the unique fact of His birth (the Incarnation) as we behold the unique fact of His death (the Atonement). In this scene, we see the instrument for the Incarnation and the instrument of the Atonement.

This is a portrait where we see everything about the Christian faith that is important, essential, and gloriously true. We should place this scene in our hearts and minds and memorize it. It is perfectly powerful.

Consider and Comment:

1. Read and re-read the verse for today. Say it in your own words.

2. How is the Doctrine of the Incarnation pictured in these two verses?

3. How is the Doctrine of the Atonement seen here?

X

Alone

Yet you are he who took me from the womb;
you made me trust you at my mother's breasts.
On you was I cast from my birth,
and from my mother's womb you have been my God. (vs. 9–10)
Be not far from me, for trouble is near,
and there is none to help. (vs. 11)
Many bulls encompass me;
strong bulls of Bashan surround me. (vs. 12)

JESUS PRAYED PSALM 22 AS HIS OWN; he embodied the entirety of it. He did not just mean the first verse and the last line. He might have prayed it in a still, small voice that could not have been heard by those gathered around the spectacle. He might never have audibly spoken a single word after He cried out the first verse. But it seems that every line and every thought refers to everything that happened on Good Friday.

The four Gospels of Matthew, Mark, Luke, and John are amazing records of the life of Christ. These different authors have different styles from one another. Some of Jesus's stories in one of the Gospels are missing in another. Those that have stories and episodes in common have them in a slightly different order. They are all different.

However, all of them have one thing in common that might be missed by the casual reader. All four Gospels are back-weighted the same. They all feature the last week in Jerusalem, the death of Jesus on the Cross, and the appearances of Risen Christ far more than any other event. They all do the same thing. The bulk of their chapters are the retelling of the last week of Jesus's life, the last three days of His life, and the last three hours of His life on the Cross.

This is instructive for us. We praise Jesus for His compassion. We are impressed with His teaching. We are amazed with His miracles. We are moved by His example. But these are not the reasons why Jesus came into the world. He came into the world to save sinners,[17] and to do that, He would have to die.

Now, in verse 11, Jesus cries out to God again; He pleads for Him to not be far. And then He adds two thoughts: *"for trouble is near"* and *"for there is none to help."*

There is a sense of sadness in these verses. Jesus had cried out to God and wondered why He seemed so far away. And now, looking around Himself, Jesus sees that there is no one to help Him. For the first time in His life, Jesus is alone. I cannot think of a single instance in His life and ministry when Jesus was ever as alone as He is now.

We are told early on that Jesus had a remarkable charisma about Him. We do not know if He was attractive by modern shallow standards, but we do know that he attracted people by the hundreds. Crowds were constantly following Him. They were often pressing in on Him. In one instance, a crowd was gathered around Jesus as He stood near a shoreline. To get closer to Him, to see and to touch Him, the crowd began pressing Him and moving Him further and further to the shoreline. He was running out of land to stand on! They were so close to Him, and He was so close to the shore, that He had to quickly hop on board the nearest boat to keep from getting pushed back into the water![18]

After Jesus was baptized in the Jordan, He was driven to the desert to be alone for 40 days. Maybe we think He was alone then. But even then, He was not alone. The Scriptures tell us that both angels and animals came to minister to Him. Even then, He was in the company of those a degree higher than humans (angels) and creatures of a degree lower than humanity (animals).

But now, on the Cross, He is alone, and from the sound of the psalm, He is on His own. He has never been so alone. No one has ever been so alone.

CONSIDER AND COMMENT:

1. Why are most of the Gospels focused on the last three days of Jesus's life?

2. Why do you think that Jesus was so popular and charismatic?

3. Jesus was never so alone as on the Cross. Comment on this fact.

XI

Bulls

Be not far from me, for trouble is near,
and there is none to help. (vs. 11)
Many bulls encompass me;
strong bulls of Bashan surround me. (vs. 12)
They open wide their mouths at me,
like a ravening and roaring lion. (vs. 13)

YES, THERE IS NO ONE TO HELP. Jesus has said this in verse 11. But, as it turns out, this does not mean there aren't people around Him. There are others. Psalm 22 depicts Him surrounded by some devilish adversaries who have established an offensive ring around him. This is the sense of verse 12, and it is as frightening as a nightmare.

Most of the people standing around the Cross would not have been mourners or sympathizers. There were evil people who confidently sprayed insults and jeers at our Lord on the Cross. These men were mean-spirited; they were vicious, and their sole purpose was to intimidate the Crucified One and to watch over the execution procedures so that the man would certainly die.

Psalm 22:12–13 anticipated this scene and called these men oxen and bulls, both horned animals that can charge forward. These are *"the strong bulls of Bashan."* They were stamping their feet, snorting, and sounding off. They were restless and ready to charge. There is a strong memory of Bashan in the Old Testament. Bashan, an area in modern-day Syria, is like a land of giants. Everything there was bigger than life and even eviler. This is part of the history of Israel. *"And the rest of Gilead, and all Bashan, being the kingdom of Og, gave I unto the half-tribe of Manasseh; all the region of Argob, with all Bashan, which was called the land of giants."[19]* These men are giant, fat bulls.

We said earlier that we know who these men were. We are certain of it. Matthew tells us specifically of their rank, position, and ferocity: *"… the chief priests mocking him, with the scribes and elders, said, He saved others; himself he cannot save. If he is the King of Israel, let him now come down from the Cross, and we will believe him. He trusted in God; let him deliver him now if he will have him: for he said, I am the Son of God."* (Matthew 27:41–43)

We do not know how many were there encircling the Cross, but they formed somewhat of a circle around the Cross. There were at least 80 men of rank in the Temple. And they were likely dressed in their massive colored coats, robes and headdresses, and other religious accoutrements signifying their high office. They are the fat religious leaders that have been eating sumptuously on fine food and wine in the Temple for years. They are experts in the Law; they know the Prophets; they do everything by the book.

The scene is truly nightmarish. The Cross is encompassed, circled, by nearly 80 large fat men with headdresses (shaped like animal horns?).

The bulls of Bashan are large religious bullies.

This ghoulish scene around the Cross is an indictment of every single part of human civilization both then and now. His followers and disciples turned away. The Roman government, which had successfully led armies to conquer the known world, could not get their act together. There was no justice; their leaders were corrupt puppets and conmen. The religious establishment colluded with the power of the state to execute a known innocent man. The crowd was angry and impulsive. Judas, a close friend and follower, betrayed Him. And one of his closest friends, Peter, denied even knowing Him.

Again, the pernicious question surfaces: What about me? Where would I stand? What would I say? Would I even speak up?

One of the most tragic statements in the New Testament is this: *"He came to that which was His own, but His own did not receive Him."*[20] Think of the enormity of humanity's crime against divinity. Jesus came to the people He loved and the world that He had made.

But instead of welcoming Him as a Savior and honoring Him as the Lord, they turned against Him.

Consider and Comment:

1. Everyone is standing in opposition to Jesus, especially the religious authorities. Why do you think this is?

2. What is nightmarish about this scene on Calvary?

3. Every part of society turned against Jesus. How and why?

XII

Evil

THERE IS AN EVIL POWER AT WORK at Calvary to get Jesus killed. This evil power of Satan has been trying to kill Jesus for years. The devil attacked Jesus in the Judean wilderness trying to trick Him into taking a spiritual shortcut to power and fame. The gospels tell us that when the devil gave up on these failed attacks, he withdrew to a more opportune time.[21]

There were other opportune times to come, for sure.

There was the first sermon Jesus preached in Nazareth.[22] It was so startling and offensive to the hearers that they rushed Jesus to the edge of a cliff to throw him over, but He easily slipped through the angry congregation.

There was a dangerous storm on the Sea of Galilee that might have been used by the devil to drown Him.[23] He calmed it. And Jesus was politically wise, so when the religious or political heat was high, and authorities were out to find him and arrest him, Jesus would withdraw for a time.[24]

He was not afraid of the devil. He confronted him by name. He cast him away many times. He exercised His superiority over him and exorcised him from others time and time again. And Jesus knew that His adversary would be most likely to try to take Him on in Jerusalem, the center of religious and local political power. But Jesus would take the devil on at a time and place of our Lord's own choosing.

Until then, the forces of evil were poisoning the people and priests. In this verse, the psalm compares them to people around the Cross as lions, with open mouths that are hungry; that roar like lions.

The animal metaphors in these two verses are very telling, and they give us further insight into the heart of Jesus—into what He is feeling. First, the horned oxen. These beasts pull sleds of heavy material and stones. Oxen were instrumental in moving the massive stones to build the Temple. There would have been hundreds of oxen around Jerusalem. The strong, fat bulls of Bashan are, as we have been told, huge. They are fat. They are well-fed. They can stamp their hooves and charge. They are dangerous.

And lastly, here are the hungry lions. They are the most vicious of all. When the Bible gives a specific warning about Satan, it describes him in the form of a lion. Peter, who knew personally the power of the devil, would later write to the scattered Christians of the early Church: *"Be sober, be watchful, your adversary, the devil is prowling around like a roaring lion. Resist him, firm in your faith."*[25]

These three animal metaphors tell us something about the nature of evil that we should know. Indeed, these two verses can serve as a final warning about the evil that has coalesced around the Cross. There are types of evil that, like the ox, will slowly and steadily push or pull us into sin. There is a kind of evil, like the strong, fat bulls, that can charge or chase us into sin. And then there is a kind of evil that, like the lion, will simply pounce and devour.

C.S. Lewis wrote, *"Good and evil both increase at compound interest. That is why the little decisions you and I make every day are of such infinite importance. The smallest, good act today is the capture of a strategic point from which, a few months later, you may be able to go on to victories you never dreamed of. An apparently trivial indulgence in lust or anger today is the loss of a ridge or railway line or bridgehead from which the enemy may launch an attack otherwise impossible."*[26]

We have been warned.

1. Why did the devil have such a vested interest in killing Jesus?

2. Compare and contrast the three kinds of animals and the three kinds of evil.

3. Underline one phrase or sentence that stands out in this chapter. Why does it?

XIII

Man

*They open wide their mouths at me,
like a ravening and roaring lion. (vs. 13)*
**I am poured out like water,
and all my bones are out of joint;
my heart is like wax;
it is melted within my breast. (vs. 14)**
*My strength is dried up like a potsherd,
and my tongue sticks to my jaws;
you lay me in the dust of death. (vs. 15)*

DO YOU NOTICE HOW MANY ASPECTS of the human body are under physical assault in this verse and the next? Jesus has endured the searing pain of the nails as his weight is pulled against his spiked wrists. He has struggled to breathe. He has been terribly traumatized. This is torture.

As the psalm begins, Jesus was assaulted by the mere thought of being forsaken, left alone, and abandoned. He prayed empty cries to empty skies. Various places in the psalm have described the deep spiritual hurt, emotional duress, and psychological pain of His trauma. These assaults are non-physical. But now, in verse 14, we are told of the terrible assault on the human body.

As Jesus recollected this 1,000-year-old psalm, He would remember the parts of His anatomy and physical being mentioned. His bones were out of joint; His heart was like melted wax. One translation says that His heart was melting, it was seeping into His bowels, His physical strength had dried up, His tongue was swollen in His dry mouth, and He was facing the dust of his death. It seems to me that these are all descriptions of the opening phrase: *"I am poured out like water..."* Is blood draining from His body?

This verse is a terrifying description of a terrible moment. And it is happening to Jesus in real-time. Our eternal God is being tortured and killed on a Cross. When we say it that way—the eternal Creator meeting His death at the hands of His creatures—we have to admit the impossibility of it all. This cannot be happening. But sadly, it is.

And even more profoundly: It had to happen. Jesus had to die.

The Christian faith holds two truths to be self-evident from the Gospel records of the life of Jesus. First, He was God Incarnate. He was the divine Son of God, descended from on High to live our life. He was born of a virgin and therefore untainted with the sin of humanity. He is the eternal second member of the Trinity. Jesus is God Incarnate.

There is another truth that Christians must believe. Jesus is also a man, a fully human being. He was born through a human birth canal. He was raised as a child of parents in a human family. He went through his childhood, learned to read and write, memorized the Scriptures, and, in His early adult years, learned a trade as a craftsman. He was a man.

These are both true: Jesus is God. Jesus is Man.

We see the two natures of Jesus Christ depicted in Psalm 22. On the Cross, we can see our Lord's physicality, the human pain and suffering from the taunts and torture. As a man, He does not have an escape plan; He does not rise above the pain and agony and retreat into some spiritual realm. The pain was excruciating, a word that actually means "to crucify."

But also, on the Cross, we see His Divinity. He continues to trust in His ever-close relationship with His Father. When He dies, we see the surrounding order jolt and rock. The earth shakes. Darkness descends. At His death, the heavy curtain protecting the Holy of Holies in the Temple was torn in two. We are not privy to everything that transpired around His death, but it was intense.

Christians have meditated and contemplated the death of Jesus for 2,000 years. There are endless truths to know and to discover in the record of his last hours. In the Gospel of Mark, the manner in which He died convinced the centurion in charge of the execution that He was the Son of God.[27]

As we read, pray, study, and think about the way our Lord Jesus died, it changes the way we want to live.

CONSIDER AND COMMENT:

1. How are the truths of Jesus the Man and also the Son of God self-evident in the Scriptures?

2. Why are these two truths critical to the Christian faith?

3. Read the account of how the centurion came to faith (Mark 15:34). What would have convinced him of Jesus's divinity?

XIV

Dust

I am poured out like water,
and all my bones are out of joint;
my heart is like wax;
it is melted within my breast. (vs. 14)
My strength is dried up like a potsherd,
and my tongue sticks to my jaws;
you lay me in the dust of death. (vs. 15)
For dogs encompass me;
a company of evildoers encircles me;
they have pierced my hands and feet—
I can count all my bones—
they stare and gloat over me. (vs. 16–17)

THE PSALM CHRONICLES THE SCENE of the
crucifixion with unbelievable accuracy. As Jesus remembers it and recites it line after line, it turns out to be happening in real-time around Him and within Him. Jesus
is exhausted. He is dehydrated. Our Victim on the Cross
is dying from multiple assaults and traumas including a
desperate lack of water. In this verse alone, we see the
traumatic conditions are applied to His strength (dried
up like a potsherd), His tongue (He cannot speak for the
dryness in His mouth), and the surrounding dust.

As we read this account, we see that Jesus did not "rise above" the suffering and severity like some sort of demi-god. His pain was as real for Him as it would have been for us.

His condition aroused the pity of someone in the crowd. A man soaked a sponge with myrrh and cheap Roman vinegar wine, put it on the end of a stick, and hoisted it up to the lips of our Lord.[28] The mixture was drugged wine intended to help victims endure their suffering. Jesus refused. He wanted to stay alert and clear. Jesus refused to drink anything that would have dulled His senses.

Later on, when He was nearing the last of His breaths, He was offered a sponge filled with only vinegar.[29] He welcomed the sponge as it pressed against his lips. He sucked in a drink. The acidic vinegar cleared His throat and allowed Him to speak His last words.

The second half of this verse is astounding: *"and you lay me in the dust of death."* We should read this verse closely and understand the magnitude of what is being said by it.

First, it describes death with the metaphor of dust. This is familiar to almost every Jew or Christian. The physical end of our physical bodies is dust. This is the fate of every human as decreed by God: *"You are dust, and to dust, you shall return."*[30]

I have presided over many interment services. It is

always a privilege to be with a grieving family for the final placement of the remains of their loved one. Every time I pick up the small box containing the final ashes of their loved ones, most of the family gasps. It is a shock to see how the fearfully and wonderfully made body of a living man or woman or child is reduced to a small container of ashes. It is sobering. This is the dust of death.

But a closer look at the verse brings us to a startling truth. The actor of the action in the verse is God. Jesus, with this psalm in mind, is praying these words to God: *"You have brought Me to the dust of death."* This means that God sent His Son to the dust to die our death.

Jesus was an innocent man, and on Calvary, He was being unjustly executed. If we did a postmortem on the last week of Jesus's life, we would find that there is plenty of blame to go around. The indictments would begin with Judas, who betrayed the Son of God into the hands of the Romans. The close friends of Jesus ran from His side. Peter denied Him. The fickle crowd turned against Him and called for His execution. The Roman government was so corrupt it was powerless to do the right thing. The religious authorities were in a deep state of division, compromise, and corruption. Indictments can be handed down to all.

But the last half of verse 15 tells us something more. Even though there were plenty of people to blame for the way the week went down, it was God the Father who sent His Son to the Cross. The executioners murdered Jesus. We can say that for sure. But we can also say that God sent Him to be killed.

It begs the question: Why?

CONSIDER AND COMMENT:

1. As we consider the reality of Jesus's death, have you reflected on your own? How?

2. Have you ever attended an interment service? What thoughts did you have then?

3. Why is it important to think about the death of Jesus? What value is there in that?

XV

Pierced

My strength is dried up like a potsherd,
and my tongue sticks to my jaws;
you lay me in the dust of death. (vs. 15)
For dogs encompass me;
a company of evildoers encircles me;
they have pierced my hands and feet—
I can count all my bones—
they stare and gloat over me. (vs. 16–17)
They divide my garments among them,
and for my clothing they cast lots. (vs. 18)

IF VERSES 16–17 IN PSALM 22 WERE ALL we had, we would know enough to understand what is happening to our Lord. The reference to piercing the hands and feet makes it clear that Psalm 22 is referencing a crucifixion as the means of death. The details of the crucifixion are hideous and its effect on the human body is catastrophic, and Jesus would have known all of this beforehand. Perhaps it was this part of Psalm 22 that he had in his mind as he sweated drops of blood in the Garden of Gethsemane on Thursday evening.[31]

Jesus knew Psalm 22 from a very early age, and in His

younger years, He would have recited it in worship and in His study. Gradually, He came to know that this psalm would pertain to Him and the manner of the death He would die. Psalm 22 was a predictive text for Him. It told Him what was going to take place. I cannot think of another historical instance where someone was aware of the means of their death long before they died.

Verse 17 is a stunning verse: *"They pierced my hands and my feet."* King David penned this psalm ten centuries before Jesus recites it, but, as I have mentioned, this phrase never could have occurred to him were it not for the inspiration of the Holy Spirit. The early church believed, as Jesus had taught, that King David was not only the past King of Israel, but a prophet and, in other psalms, foretold the resurrection of Jesus Christ.[32]

Crucifixion was invented by the Persians in the 4th century BC and is still regarded as the most extreme form of torture ever devised. The victim does not die from the wounds inflicted by the nails. (It is likely that the wrists or arms were bound to the crossbeam with ropes.) Rather, the weight of the body does not allow for breathing; a man suffocates from crucifixion. The nails function only to pin the victim to the cross and take away every means of protection or survival.

Psalm 22:17 tells us about the outward appearance of the crucified man. Most common paintings of the torture of Jesus show Him stretched out on the Cross, His arms fully opened, and His torso extended. The artists also cover Him with a loincloth for modesty. But there was no modesty on Calvary. He was fully naked, stripped of any article of clothing, and, in the midst of His agony, He looked down at His distended body and realized that this unique detail of the psalm was also being fulfilled.

The evil intent of these crimes turned out for the glory of God. The nail marks in the hands of the Risen Christ became sure proof that the Early Church needed to believe that He had Risen. These nail marks, the ones in His hands or wrists, His feet, and the wound created in His side were the emblem of His victory. Jesus readily showed these wounds to His disciples. When one of them (Thomas) was absent that night, Jesus returned the following week to show the doubting disciple the beautiful proofs of His death and so prove His Resurrection.[33]

It is very interesting to note that Jesus's Resurrection body bore the visible marks of the Crucifixion. His body was made new in every way we can think of. He could appear in a room behind locked doors, yet He was not a ghost. He could walk, talk, and eat with His disciples but also could simply disappear and reappear somewhere else. He had what the Apostle Paul would refer later to as a *"spiritual body."* But the marks of the nails were never repaired or covered, and, for the Early Church, they became the proof that the Risen Christ they saw with their eyes was the same man that had been on the Cross.

Whatever evil had been meted out by the executioners was intended for good, for the saving of many.

Consider and Comment:

1. Have you ever thought that Jesus knew this level of detail about His death? What thoughts or feelings do you have about it?

2. Underline one phrase or sentence in this chapter. Why did you choose it?

3. Why did the Resurrected body of Jesus show the marks of His crucifixion?

XVI

Garments

For dogs encompass me;
a company of evildoers encircles me;
they have pierced my hands and feet—
I can count all my bones—
they stare and gloat over me. (vs. 16–17)
They divide my garments among them,
and for my clothing they cast lots. (vs. 18)
But you, O LORD, do not be far off!
O you my help, come quickly to my aid! (vs. 19)

AS WE HAVE SEEN, nearly every aspect of Psalm 22 applied to the experience of our Lord on Calvary. Jesus knew the entire psalm by heart, and as He quietly recited it, the scenes it described were played out at ground level around Him. This is true even for the minute level of detail that we read in verse 18. The psalm mentions, of all things, His robe.

There was a reason why the guards were casting lots for Jesus's clothing. There were some pieces of some of it that could be distributed among a few of them. After all, laying hold of the personal effects of any condemned man were perquisites that came with the job.

However, one article of clothing drew special attention because it was large and seamless. (These details are given to us in the Gospel of John.)[34] The guards decided to gamble for the robe rather than cut it up among themselves.

When we read the accounts of the Passion, the hours of Jesus's crucifixion, the four Gospel writers give us details of how it took place. We are told who is near the Cross and who fled. We are told who cursed Jesus. We are told how a few of the crowd took pity on our Lord in his final hours and offered him water. And we are told that Jesus spoke seven times during those hours. These sayings have been collected as "The Seven Last Words of Christ." Not all of them are found in every Gospel record of His last hours, but every record has at least one of His last words. Luke has three of them. John records three. And Matthew and Mark have one each and it is the same one from Psalm 22.

These are the seven words of Christ from the Cross:

- *My God, my God, why have you forsaken me?*

- *I thirst.*

- *Woman, behold your son; son, behold your mother. (to Mary and John)*

- *Father forgive them; they do not know what they are doing.*

- *Today, you will be with me in paradise. (to a thief next to him)*

- *Father, into your hands I commit my spirit.*

- *It is finished.*

These seven statements are worthy of deep thought and meditation all by themselves. We often meditate on them in Holy Week one by one. However, taken as a whole, they show us something that is critical to know about Jesus's last hours. This man, though beaten, terrorized, ridiculed, and pierced, is fully and mentally awake. He has his wits about Him. He is cognizant of everything that is taking place.

When Jesus looks beneath the Cross, He sees some soldiers gambling for the only thing of value that was His. He knows He has been stripped clean of everything. He has nothing left to call His own. Did He remember the proverb He spoke from His earlier years? *"Foxes have holes, the birds of the air have nests, but the Son of Man has no place to lay his head."* [35] He was homeless and naked.

All of us come into the world naked. And, like it or not, we will all ultimately be naked again, at the last. This is Job's conclusion: *"Naked came I out of my mother's womb, and naked shall I return there: The Lord gave, and the Lord has taken away; blessed be the name of the Lord."* [36]

There is one more last thing Jesus said that is recorded in the Gospel. There is, if you will, an eighth "Word from the Cross." It is mentioned in the Gospel of Mark.

"And Jesus uttered a loud cry and breathed his last. And the curtain of the temple was torn in two, from top to bottom. And when the centurion, who stood facing him, saw that in this way he breathed his last, he said, 'Truly this man was the Son of God!'" [37]

Jesus's last word on the Cross was actually a loud cry. We do not know what He said, but it contained vast emotion. Was it a relief? Was it a release? We do not know. But it was enough to bring the captain of the guard to faith. He is the first person to be converted by the death of Jesus. He would not be the last.

Consider and Comment:

1. Of these Seven Last Words of Jesus, which are the most powerful or moving to think about?

2. Jesus seems to be trying to stay aware and cognizant of things around Him. Why do you think this is?

3. What is your reaction to Job's comments quoted above?

XVII

Wrath

They divide my garments among them,
and for my clothing they cast lots. (vs. 18)
But you, O LORD, do not be far off!
O you my help, come quickly to my aid! (vs. 19)
Deliver my soul from the sword,
my precious life from the power of the dog!
Save me from the mouth of the lion!
You have rescued me from the horns
of the wild oxen! (vs. 20–21)

———

JUST 24 HOURS BEFORE THE CRUCIFIXION
took place, Jesus arrived at the Garden of Gethsemane
with His disciples to pray. Once there, He moved to
a place about a stone's throw from them and began a
deep heart-to-heart prayer with the Father. He pleaded,
"Father, if it is possible, please let this cup pass me by."
What is the cup was He talking about?

"The cup" is an Old Testament allusion to a vessel of
some sort that is meant to hold a measure of something.
In this case of Jesus's garden prayer, "the cup" referred
to a "cup of wrath" that God was ready to pour out over
all of Israel for their sins and offenses.[38] Shockingly,

Jesus was going to take this cup of wrath on Himself. He had willingly accepted this role from His Father and agreed to receive the full measure of the wrath of God for the sins of the world.

There are mysteries in the Christian faith that lie beyond the grasp of our intellect. This is difficult for modern people to accept; we like to bring science in to address an unknown. But that does not work with God. If we could answer every question, faith would be unneeded. God says in Isaiah:

> *…my thoughts are not your thoughts,*
> *neither are your ways my ways, declares the Lord.*
> *For as the heavens are higher than the earth,*
> *so are my ways higher than your ways*
> *and my thoughts than your thoughts.*[39]

We should consider this carefully when we think about the wrath of God and the "cup of wrath." After all, what is the wrath of God? Is it a character defect in God that He bears so much wrath? This is especially hard to understand because modern believers love to talk about love, God's love. Any discussion of wrath is bound to be off-putting.

God's wrath or anger is His divine reaction to sin. It is not His response to us, per se, but to our sin. God's nature and our sin are so incompatible that His response to sin is wrath. God's righteous wrath is the consequence of sin. Michael Green has said that wrath is "God's settled opposition to all that is evil." Honestly, this is what we would want of God. We would not want Him to forget about evil, look the other way, or minimize it in any way. All of us want a maximal divine response to sin; again, not to us, but to our sin.

The Bible often speaks in metaphors to help us to understand complex mysteries. In this case, God's wrath is in a cup, a cup that Jesus agrees to drink into himself in the Garden, and the same cup that He drinks on the Cross.

This means that Jesus was willing to take on the holy wrath of a holy God; He chose to become the figurehead for all of Israel as He took the full measure of the wrath of God into Himself. Returning to the metaphor of Light and Darkness, it was as if Jesus became the Darkness that God's Light must dispel.

We do not fully understand these things from a human viewpoint, but we can see this looming question on nearly every page of the Bible: How can these sinful people (Darkness) be reconciled to a Holy God (Light)? Jesus was the answer.

Verse 19 is a cry from Jesus. It is a request for help and aid to do the thing He has agreed to do. To drink the cup of the wrath of God. This cry of Jesus is a request, if possible, to spare Him.

Jesus, though very reluctant to take it on, never asked

to be relieved from the Cross. Jesus was committed to take on the sins of the entire world and allow God His Father to expel His wrath and expunge the record of our sins.

These are deep thoughts, and they should move us. Most modern people do not understand why sin is such a serious problem for God. That is because of the hardness of our hearts. But sin produces divine wrath in God the Father.

And Jesus took it upon Himself to take it all upon Himself.

CONSIDER AND COMMENT:

1. As stated above, the divine wrath is "God's settled opposition to all that is evil." What is your reaction to this statement?

2. What is "the cup" that Jesus is hesitant to take in the Garden?

3. Why is sin such a serious problem for God?

XVIII

Answer

NOW, AFTER SEVERAL HOURS OF PRAYER and petition to His Father, while enduring deep suffering and pain, Jesus speaks a final word of prayer to be delivered. He is near the end, and he petitions God to deliver His soul, His life.

The crowd continues to chastise our Lord, but the war is nearly over. There is a final battle, yes, but the outcome of the war has been determined. It is all over but the dying.

A victorious new life will miraculously follow. We can remember the words of Thomas Aquinas who said that Jesus was a "saving victim" which sounds like an oxymoron. But it is accurate. A modern writer, Frederick

Buechner used the phrase "magnificent defeat." It is both.

Verses 20–21 are the last petitions of our Lord from the Cross. He refers to the mockers and accusers by the animal names we have already studied. Jesus tells us of two more threats to His life and His soul. He asks to be delivered from the sword and from the horns of wild oxen, images that both refer to severe, piercing wounds.

Less than 24 hours earlier, in the Garden of Gethsemane, Jesus had been captured by sword-bearing soldiers. There was a scuffle between Peter and some of the squad leaders of the arresting party. Peter drew his sword and injured a servant of the high priest, but Jesus healed the man and rebuked Peter for even drawing his sword. The sword is the symbol of political power and military might, and it should have no place in the work of His disciples.[40]

Jesus did not only disarm His disciples—He disarmed himself, too. Jesus possessed vast power and He demonstrated this throughout His ministry. But not now. He told the disciples in the Garden of Gethsemane that He could, at any moment, appeal to His Father to dispatch an entire legion of angels to do His bidding. But now, on the Cross, He is defenseless. He has surrendered everything.

Hebrew names of animals and beasts are notoriously difficult to translate. But whatever specific beasts are mentioned in these verses, it is clear they are a dangerous threat. There are also some grammatical issues in the Hebrew that inform how we understand this section of the psalm. In some versions, verse 21 reads this way: *"Save Me from the lion's mouth and from the horns of the wild oxen! You have answered Me."* Other translations have adjusted it to read, *"Save me from the mouth of the lion. You have rescued me from the hands of the wild oxen."* "Answered" and "rescued" are the same word.

Some translations of this verse remove all doubt that the time of prayer is over. They read, *"And He answered me!"* Jesus does not offer another petition or plea after verse 21.

Regardless of how we translate the verse, there is a definite sense of turning in the psalm at this point. It appears that after hours of petitioning, Jesus knows that God has answered His prayer. Jesus has a strong belief that all will be well because God has answered Him.

He has been granted the answer to His prayer, and He is ready to praise God and declare His name widely. His circumstances have not changed. He is still dying. The nail spikes are still shot through his wrists, the steel still buried deep in the timber of the Cross.

But praise, thanksgiving, victory, hope, and joy are filling our Lord's mind as He continues to pray through the verses of Psalm 22.

CONSIDER AND COMMENT:

1. Why did Jesus disarm his disciples in the Garden of Gethsemane?

2. Does your translation of Psalm 22:20–21 read like an answer has been given to Jesus?

3. Underline the most important sentence in this chapter. Why did you choose it?

XIX

Interlude

*Deliver my soul from the sword,
my precious life from the power of the dog!
Save me from the mouth of the lion!
You have rescued me from
the horns of the wild oxen! (vs. 20–21)*
**I will tell of your name to my brothers;
in the midst of the congregation I will praise you. (vs. 22)**

THERE IS AN ANCIENT PRAYER of the Church that was written in 10th century AD by a colorfully named saint, St. Notker the Stammerer.[41] (He had a speech impediment.) His prayer is well known to any ordained minister in a liturgical tradition. It is intoned as part of solemn collects (prayers) during the Office of the Burial of the Dead. It is simple and profound: *In the midst of life, we are in death.* We know this means that as we live our lives, build our careers, raise families, and grow old, we are, at any point, one step away from our death. We do not know when death is coming, but we are certain that it is. Every day takes us one step closer to the moment we will go down to the dust of death. This subject might have been the theme of Psalm 22:1–21.

However, the second section of Psalm 22 (verses 22–31) takes us in nearly the opposite direction. Jesus embodies the words of the psalm to say, in effect: *"In the midst of death, we are in life!"* This is part of the surprising joy of Psalm 22. Far from being a declaration of doom, when taken as a whole, the psalm is vastly encouraging. The Psalm on the Cross begins in the darkness and ends in the light of hope and praise.

We will see a complete change of aspect in Psalm 22 between verse 21 and 22. The poetic narrative has been hard to read and hard to hear. But from verse 22 to the end, there is a growing optimism, joy, and triumph about the final victory that is achieved through the Cross. After 21 verses, we encounter hope and promise; we find reasons to celebrate and join in congregational worship, and confidence that the message of God's love will go forth throughout the world.

This is the Good News found everywhere in the New Testament. Paul will say it in various ways. He wrote to the Romans: *"For I consider that the sufferings of this present time are not worth comparing with the glory that is to be revealed to us."*[42]

He wrote to the Christians at Corinth: *"For our light and momentary troubles are achieving for us an eternal glory that far outweighs them all. So, we fix our eyes not on what is seen, but on what is unseen, since what is seen is temporary, but what is unseen is eternal."*[43]

Even in the Book of Revelation, the terrifying visions that dominate the mid-section of the book are replaced by a most hopeful and powerful promise of the life and the world to come. *"And I heard a loud voice from the throne saying, 'Behold, the dwelling place of God is with man. He will dwell with them, and they will be his people, and God himself will be with them as their God. He will wipe away every tear from their eyes, and death shall be no more, neither shall there be mourning, nor crying, nor pain anymore, for the former things have passed away.'"* [44]

These last verses in Psalm 22 must have been a balm to Jesus. They would have given Him aid and comfort through the long hours of suffering. As mentioned earlier, His victory was always sure. The war was over. But still there remained the dying.

Haven't you experienced this? Haven't you glimpsed some light, even though you might still suffer in dark and difficult times? Without ever denying the reality of pain and disappointment in our lives, we often can feel a fresh wind of strength and hope come upon us. We call it seeing "light at the end of the tunnel." Praise the Lord for this.

So now we turn to these nine verses to discover what hope and promise they can bring from the devastating torture of our Lord. And we will find that our hope, our unshakable hope both in the present and in eternity, is in the Cross of our Lord Jesus Christ.

1. What is your reaction to St. Notker's prayer and Jesus's experience on the Cross?

2. Have you ever experienced a fresh wind of hope and strength in a time of difficulty?

3. Paraphrase both of St. Paul's quotes above. Which one seems more relevant to your life today?

XX

Congregation

*I will tell of your name to my brothers;
in the midst of the congregation I will praise you. (vs. 22)*

AS WE ENTER VERSE 22, our vision expands from the scene of the Cross and we see something new: faithful people who gather to praise and worship the Lord!

The scene of the psalm takes us inside a worship service. Worship, of course, was an essential element of David's life. The emotion in many of his psalms shows us that David absolutely loved to worship God. Once, as is famously known, David was so exuberantly glad to worship the Lord that he danced publicly, to the dismay of his wife.[45] The worship of Almighty God was at the center of Israel's life in the ancient world. There are very few times in the Old Testament when we read about private worship. Rather, worship is a corporate action before God.

When Jesus applied this psalm to himself as He hung on the Cross, He might have imagined the joy of fellowship and worship that He and His band of disciples and followers enjoyed in the early days of ministry. This corporate gathering continued after the Resurrection as well. The disciples continued to meet together, and the early church cemented this "worship together" ethos as an indelible part of the life of a Christian. The Book of Hebrews instructs us to ensure that we are *not giving up meeting together, as some are in the habit of doing, but to encourage one another—and all the more as you see the Day approaching."* [46]

In contrast, our modern church often emphasizes individual relationships with God and personal faith in Jesus. While important, those categories are not often considered in the New Testament church. Just as the psalm says, *"In the midst of the congregation will I praise you,"* the church is to be a gathered group. We are to remember the first command of the risen Christ, *"Go to the others."* [47]

Christianity is not a solo sport. *"I will tell of your name to my brothers,"* prayed Christ on the Cross.

After His resurrection, the early Christians became well known for their gatherings. On Pentecost, fifty days after the Resurrection, they continued their regular meetings, but now publicly. These gatherings were so impressive and so attractive to others that the new church grew exponentially. We read in the Book of Acts that the brothers and sisters *continued in the Apostle's teaching, the fellowship, the breaking of bread, and the prayers."* And then we are told, *"...the Lord added to their number daily those who were being saved."* [48]

Meeting and worshiping together is the dominant

ethos of the church. To be a congregation is to congregate, to gather around a central cause: the worship and praise of our God in heaven. The Greek word translated "church" in the New Testament is *ekklesia,* the literal translation of which is "a called-out assembly."

Even as I write this chapter, the COVID-19 pandemic is, in many places, forcing the people of God to operate opposite of the very core of what it means to be the gathered, worshiping church.

When King David wrote verse 22, he had the ancient Israelite congregation in mind. When Jesus applies the verse to Himself, He has the church in mind. His church! He thinks about the holy assembly, the congregation of believers, the gathering of God's faithful people, and He cannot wait to be in their midst.

In a sense, Jesus cannot wait to come to church!

CONSIDER AND COMMENT:

1. What is your response to the passage from Hebrews 10:25?

2. How important is congregational worship to you and your faith?

3. When the pandemic prevented or limited in-person worship, how did you maintain your faith without being able to gather with your congregation?

XXI

Awe

You who fear the LORD, praise him!
All you offspring of Jacob, glorify him,
and stand in awe of him, all you offspring of Israel! (vs. 23)

FOR THE FIRST TIME, the words of the psalm are addressed to others. There is hope!

In the first section of Psalm 22, the plaintiff is speaking to God. *"Why have you..."* and *"But you are holy..."* and *"Our fathers trusted in you..."* Then, as the psalm continues, Jesus describes His physical, spiritual, emotional state. *"I am poured out like water..."* and *"My strength is dried up..."* and *"I will declare Your name..."*

In a sense, the first section of the psalm reads like a personal journal, an intimate description of the agonies of the Cross. Now, in verse 23, the audience expands. Jesus speaks to different groups and tells them to glorify and praise the Lord.

If we look closely, we can see that there are three different groups of people that Jesus would have had in mind: those who *"fear the Lord,"* those who are the *"offspring of Jacob,"* and those who are *"the offspring of Israel."* The first group is summoned to praise Him, the second is told to glorify Him, and the third group is called to "stand in awe of Him."

Who are these groups of believers? Obviously, there is a lot of overlap between these three groups, but the differences provide wonderful depth to the psalm and what might have been in the heart of our Lord on the Cross.

Those who simply *"fear the Lord"* are not afraid of God! "Fear" at this point in the psalm means awe. This type of fear is what happens when a sinner first understands the holiness and transcendent goodness of God. As we become more aware of God's holiness, we become more aware of our sinfulness. This is why, for example, when Isaiah sees the magnificent and powerful presence of the Lord filling the Temple, his first response is, *"Woe is me!"* [49] He is awestruck! That is what it means to have a "fear of the Lord"—and why the psalm tells us that praise follows fear.

The second group are the descendants of Jacob. Jacob was one of the early patriarchs, the son of Isaac and the grandson of the father of our faith, Abraham. The descendants of Jacob are people who have a long-standing faith; they have the "faith of their fathers," but it has not been tested, as Jacob in his early years had not been tested. Jacob believed in God, to be sure. But he saw his faith through his personal needs and human desires. His religion was not so much *true* for him as it was a *tool* for him. Jacob believed in the God of his fathers, but for the wrong reasons. Descendants of Jacob may have faith, but it is a light faith.

The third group are the offspring of Israel. Many readers of the Bible will know that Jacob and Israel are the same person. The key difference, however, is that Israel was said to have striven with God. Jacob is given the name of Israel after he has been tested and tried at the River Jabbok.[50] The descendants of Israel are those who have wrestled mightily with God. Their faith has been tested by adversity, and they have grown in knowledge and depth of insight. These are the true saints of God who approach the challenges of life with calmness and hard-earned wisdom.

The point of this verse is not to draw too careful of distinctions between these three groups. Rather, the point is to summon them all to the high praise of our awesome God. Each of the believers are instructed by the speaker of the psalm to praise and glorify the Lord forever.

Clearly, we are at a different place in Psalm 22 than where we started. Even though Jesus's situation has not changed, and His circumstances are still enormously difficult, He is celebrating the faithful people who believe in God and come before Him in awe with glory and praise. We now see that He, in a sense, has become a worship leader for the God whom He previously felt had turned away from Him.

CONSIDER AND COMMENT:

1. In your own words, describe the three kinds of people that are included in this verse.

2. Which of these groups can you relate to?

3. Jesus calls them all to worship and praise. How often do you respond to God with worship and praise?

XXII

Love

For he has not despised or abhorred
the affliction of the afflicted,
and he has not hidden his face from him,
but has heard, when he cried to him. (vs. 24)

THERE ARE SOME WONDERFUL TRUTHS about God that Jesus reveals to us in His psalm on the Cross. Remember, this is David's psalm that Jesus has memorized, recited, and, on the Cross on Calvary, applied to His life. He is not just praying the psalm but is living it out minute by minute.

In this verse we need to pay attention to the pronouns. Using the words first written by King David, Jesus is speaking about the attributes of God: that God has compassion on the afflicted, that God has not hidden His face from the afflicted man, and that God hears the cries of the afflicted.

Jesus is taking on the identity of the afflicted one, and God is completely present with and responsive to the afflicted one. Most particularly, God does not hide His face from him.[51]

There were questions we could not answer at the beginning of the psalm. Remember that Jesus cried out to a God who seemed as if He was not there (verses 1–2)? Was Jesus really forsaken by His Father? It seemed that way to our Lord at the time. Did the Father turn His face away and abandon Jesus on the Cross? It felt that way, at least to us as we observed it. Would God really ever turn His back on His Son? Will He ever turn His back on us?

Now we know the answer. In the end, God will never hide from the afflicted. God will never turn His face from Him. It may seem sometimes that He does. But as Jesus reflects on the true nature of God in this verse, He says that God is full of compassion. He hears us when we cry.

Psalm 22 has revealed something about Jesus that we do not see or read about anywhere else in the Bible. The Gospels give us insight into the mind of Jesus. His teaching and command of Scripture were brilliant. His work with those who were outcast, broken, forgotten, or despised is well known. He had deep compassion.

But this psalm gives us a window into the heart of our Savior. We see the depth of His dependence on God—a dependence that made it all the more shocking when God seemed to abandon Him. Yet in this verse, as in the second section of this psalm, we see that Jesus's consternation about God's inattention and lack of presence turned, once again, into deep trust.

We get a strong sense in the Gospels that Jesus loved the people around Him because He knew that God loved them. And that is true. But this psalm has provided another insight into Jesus's heart and motivation. Throughout Psalm 22, we have seen Jesus endure the agony and pain of the Cross, not only because of His *Father's* love for us, but also because of His own love for us.

Thank God for Jesus!

CONSIDER AND COMMENT:

1. The Father never turned His face away; He never turned His back on Jesus. How does this impact your understanding of the Cross?

2. How does this impact your understanding of the first verse of Psalm 22?

3. Has God revealed Himself to you in your time of need? In what way?

XXIII

Father

*From you comes my praise in the
great congregation;
my vows I will perform before
those who fear him. (vs. 25)*

THE BIBLE USES HUMAN METAPHORS and word pictures to talk about God. It must, if we humans are to understand it! We are image-oriented people, and we tend to have difficulty relating to abstractions. Models help us understand how things work. This is true on a scientific level and on a theological level.

For example, if we claim—as the Bible does—that God is good, powerful, loving, and kind, we are speaking in the abstract. These statements can be true, but what do they mean to us? To others? How can we experience these? Simply saying that God is a good, powerful, loving, and kind *Father* helps us understand. The concepts come into focus. We understand because most of us have a model of a father, good or bad, to help us understand God's role as Father.

Verse 25 continues the thinking in verse 24, creating

one complete thought. David wrote (and thus Jesus prayed) that God hears the prayers of His people. As we saw in verse 24, He does not turn away from our affliction, and He hears our cries to Him.

These are distinct ideas of how God listens to us and hears the prayers we pray. God is acting like our Father and for this reason, David/Jesus feels moved to praise Him in the great assembly; David/Jesus is ready to speak before those who fear Him in the congregation.

In Psalm 22:24–25, we have seen two "pictures" for God that help us understand Him. First, He has a face that will not turn away. And second, He has an ear that will hear. We do not imagine that God has a literal face or an ear, of course. These are metaphors for who He is and how He relates to us.

If we go back to the beginning of this journey and remember the first comments from our Lord, we see a dramatic change. Jesus was asking "Why?" in verse one, and here near the end of the psalm, Jesus feels an overwhelming connection with the Father. Perhaps a better word would be "re-connection." This is the spiritual journey of Psalm 22 as applied to Jesus. He went from pain to praise.

The first Archbishop of Canterbury of the Anglican Church was Thomas Cranmer. Among many other things, Bishop Cranmer was the principal architect and author of the Book of Common Prayer. Many of the written prayers were gathered and compiled from centuries of faithful worship. Cranmer's signature prayer is known as the Collect for Purity. As you read it, note that it takes the same position about how we are able to praise and worship God. The psalm says that praise is not something that we generate or invent on our own. Our praise of God comes from God Himself! *"From you comes my praise..."* We are too broken and sinful to offer God anything. But God creates in us a clean heart in order that we might worthily magnify the name of God. God is the object of our praise, and He provides the means for it.

Cranmer's collect is beautiful:

"Almighty God, to you all hearts are open, all desires known, and from you no secrets are hid: Cleanse the thoughts of our hearts by the inspiration of your Holy Spirit, that we may perfectly love you, and worthily magnify your holy Name; through Christ our Lord. Amen."

Did you notice it? It is God who is asked to cleanse the thoughts of our heart in order to more perfectly love Him. The psalm is making the same claim that praise for God comes from God.

CONSIDER AND COMMENT:

1. How are these two verses (24–25) important to our understanding of God and His relationship to us?

2. How does using the metaphor of "Father" for God help you understand His nature?

3. How would our prayer life be different if we believed that God has a face that will never turn away; He has an ear that will always hear?

XXIV

Satisfaction

The afflicted shall eat and be satisfied;
those who seek him shall praise the LORD!
May your hearts live forever! (vs. 26)

THIS SECTION OF OUR PSALM is teeming with good news and joy! Every single verse is telling us something hopeful and wonderful about the nature of God and our life with Him. And in verse 26, we discover yet another wonderful aspect of God's care and provision for us.

First, we see that the afflicted shall eat and find satisfaction. This is a sign of God's generous outpouring of provision. The afflicted are not given mere morsels to eat or thrown a few crumbs and told to make it on their own. A lavish banquet awaits them. They shall eat to their own fullness and satisfaction. This metaphor doesn't have the power it did in the ancient world. Our grocery stores are overstocked with food. But for thousands of years, finding enough food to eat every day was everyone's primary concern. Verse 26 promises an end to that daily frustration of hunger. There is plenty of food; enough food to be satisfied.

Jesus demonstrated this in His teaching and ministry of miraculous provision. All four Gospels record the miracle of the loaves and fish. Recall that there was a great crowd of people who had followed Jesus out into the countryside to listen to His teaching. When they grew hungry, the disciples were eager to send them away to find their own food. Jesus, however, challenged them to provide a meal for thousands of people.

When the disciples failed, Jesus miraculously provided meals for the entire assembly. The people ate until they were satisfied, and still there were basketfuls of food left over. God is not cheap or stingy!

Secondly, we learn that God's nature is *not* to hide from us. In fact, Psalm 22 shows us that those who seek Him shall find Him and then praise Him. There need be no frustration about this either. Those who seek *will* find! In fact, it is fair to say that frustration in finding God or anxiety about remaining close to God should be very rare in the life of a believer. Remember that Jesus spoke about this. The 18th-century poet Christopher Smart paraphrased one of Jesus's most famous sayings this way:

Where ask is have, where seek is find,
Where knock is open wide.

This underscores the biblical truth that God does not hide from us. If we seek Him, we will find Him. James has the same thought: *"Draw near to God and He will draw near to you."* [52]

This is why the death of Jesus brings us so much hope. Just as He, in his affliction, sought God and was satisfied, so too will we be fed by our Creator. The psalm says to those who are hungry and those who are seeking, *"May your hearts live forever!"* This is the promise of eternal life, made possible by the mercy of God through the Cross of Jesus.

Consider and Comment:

1. Which line or phrase in this chapter has something to say to you? Why?

2. How does this specific verse reflect the nature of God?

3. The miracle of the loaves and fish is the only miracle that is recorded in all four Gospel accounts. Why was this miracle so central to Jesus's ministry?

XXV

Revival

All the ends of the earth shall remember
and turn to the LORD,
and all the families of the nations
shall worship before you. (vs. 27)

DO YOU KNOW THAT JESUS never talked about His past? We have no record of Him referring to His childhood, His apprenticeship under Joseph, or His early days in ministry. He never spoke about the last year or even yesterday. Jesus was always looking at what God is doing today and what He is going to do in the future. Jesus was never nostalgic for the way things used to be. His sights were always pointed forward.

Here, on the Cross, Jesus's life was ebbing away, breath by tortured breath. But rather than dwell on the terrible injustice that had been meted out, His thoughts seemed to focus on the future: the great, glorious, and grand future of God's kingdom.

Jesus trusts that the world will remember and turn to God. This is the powerful vision of a worldwide revival of faith. Can you picture the entire world remembering

God and turning to Him? Alleluia!

But what is it that the world needs to remember? What do we need to remember? The Bible makes clear in the first few chapters of Genesis that we are created by God. There is no such thing as a "self-made" person; we were all made by God. In the history of our world, this humbling fact is often forgotten. We act as if we are master creators of all that we have. Yet this is exactly upside-down.

Isaiah pegged this self-idolatry 300 years after David wrote this psalm. He said, *You turn things upside down! Shall the potter be regarded as the clay, that the thing made should say of its maker, 'He did not make me'; or the thing formed say of him who formed it, 'He has no understanding'*? [53]

Psalm 22:27 promises a worldwide awakening, a right-ordering in which God's creation remembers that He is the Creator, and worships Him for it. People all over the globe will return to the Lord; they will be turned to the Lord.

We should notice something else here too. This worldwide revival will bring all families of the nations into this new relationship with the Lord. There is an important distinction to be made here. This new gathering of people will be organized by families, not by nations. The Bible does not forecast a spiritual "United Nations" of harmony and love. The boundaries between nations and governments are temporary. It is the families of the nations that come to worship Him.

John writes about this in Revelation. In heaven, a chorus of four-winged creatures and 24 elders worship the Lamb who had been slain. They sing to Him:

> *because you were slain,*
> *and with your blood you purchased for God*
> *Persons from every tribe and language*
> *and people and nation.*
> *You have made them to be a kingdom*
> *and priests to serve our God,*
> *and they will reign on the earth.*[54]

In this biblical vision from Revelation, all national boundaries fall away. Here is another benefit of the glorious death of Jesus Christ. The dividing walls, tribal hostilities, racial tensions, and displays of national pride are all set aside. The Kingdom is filled with people from every manmade division serving the Lord as one kingdom.

CONSIDER AND COMMENT:

1. In what ways do you try to be a "self-made" man or woman? What does that term mean to you?

2. What do you think about the comment about the United Nations?

3. How would a worldwide revival change your world? Or change you?

XXVI

Kingdom

For kingship belongs to the LORD,
and he rules over the nations. (vs. 28)

THE FACT THAT JESUS CHOSE this psalm during His time on the Cross has taught us much about His heart. This far into the psalm's 31 verses, we can know that it gave Him great comfort. Even though His circumstances were torturous—and would be so until his death—through Psalm 22 He sees that the deathly circumstances of the Cross will be transformed, in God's time. Soon, the earthly kingdom will be the Lord's.

Our world today is not ruled by the government of Jesus Christ. For reasons known only to God, Satan has been allowed to rule over this present world. He has not been given free rein, and he does not reign free. He has rather limited jurisdiction. While it may seem that Satan has unlimited roaming privileges, he cannot accomplish everything he wants. He is a chained beast; there are places he cannot go.

The Bible is clear on this point. Satan is only "allowed" to run and roam. He cannot do anything he wants;

he does not do everything he wants. When he goes head-to-head with Jesus in the New Testament, he doesn't get very far.

We see this in Jesus's temptation in the wilderness. The last temptation of Satan is to show Jesus every kingdom of the earth; he claims that they are all his. He has been granted them, and he will hand them over to Jesus if He will worship his devilish self. Satan is rebuffed firmly, however, and leaves to wait for another opportune time.

Every one of us is assaulted and buffeted by temptations daily. We are distracted and deluged so much that we can grow numb to the real evil that awaits us. Oftentimes our powers of resistance seem futile. Even the Apostle Paul wrestled with tendencies and temptations as he confessed to the Christians in Rome, *"The very thing I do not want to do, I do!"* [55] I'm sure all of us can identify with that struggle.

Yet, let us remember something: This matter is settled by the Cross. We see it in verse 28. The kingdom of earth is the Lord's, and He rules over the nations. The future does not belong to the past rulers or princes of this world. Rather, the kingdom belongs to God, and His Son will reign upon the earth. This guaranteed outcome is due to the crucifixion of Jesus Christ.

And yet we earnestly ask: Why does evil still run rampant in this world? Why does it seem that Satan is still in charge of the kingdom around us? Most of us will not like the answer Scripture gives. Even though we are under new management because of the Crucifixion, it is not yet time for this world's evil tenant to be eternally evicted. He still trashes the place, and he is way behind on his rent, but it is not the right time to oust him.

This is not the answer I want to hear. But I don't think it is far from the truth. Psalm 22:28 shows us that one day the kingdom will be under new management.

Until that day, we can do what Jesus told us to do in His most famous Sermon on the Mount: *"Seek first the Kingdom of God and his righteousness."* [56]

CONSIDER AND COMMENT:

1. How does this verse address the issues of evil in the world today?

2. How do you navigate the fact that you have been redeemed and forgiven by Christ, and yet are still active in your sin?

3. Did you underline a sentence or a phrase in this chapter? Why?

XXVII

Everyone

All the prosperous of the earth eat and worship;
before him shall bow all who go down to the dust,
even the one who could not keep himself alive. (vs. 29)

PSALM 22 IS BREAKING OPEN into a vision of the entire world entering into a relationship with a living and loving God. In this verse, we see both the high and mighty and the lowest and poorest, all summoned to praise our mighty God. This is both a beautiful image that the psalm gives us and one more glorious promise of the Cross of Christ.

Normally, in the Bible, the rich and wealthy fall under criticism and, in some places, contempt from God. We understand why. It is quite often that money and power corrupt people and institutions. That is part of the taint of original sin. Jesus had some choice things to say about those with an inflated estimation of themselves. He warned the wealthy that they should be careful to only serve one master.

Yet Jesus did not despise the wealthy of this world. In one of the most tender and transparent scenes in the

New Testament, a rich young ruler turns away from following Jesus. He chooses to keep his wealth and not follow our Lord because, as the story tells us, he had much. But even still, the story tells us that Jesus loved him.[57]

The wealthy in the world face specific challenges. In the Ephesian Church there were some wealthy members whose love of money compromised their faith. They were dependent on money for their identity and security. The Apostle Paul instructed Timothy to speak directly to the money-lovers. Paul goes on to tell Timothy that money is not the root of all evil. It was the *love* of money pushed or pulled people into sin.

For the love of money is a root of all kinds of evils. It is through this craving that some have wandered away from the faith and pierced themselves with many pangs.[58]

Even with these caveats, the Kingdom is wide enough to encompass the wealthy and prosperous of the world. The entrance may be narrow, as small as the eye of a needle,[59] but once inside, the home is big enough to be the home for anyone.

The mercy of God extends to the poor and outcast as well the rich! As we see in this verse, the mercy and love of God will cover for those who go down to the dust, a reference to the poor who, unlike the rich, live amidst the dirt and grime of a hard life. But this image also references all those who literally and finally go down to

XXVIII

Finished

Posterity shall serve him;
it shall be told of the Lord to the coming generation;
they shall come and proclaim his righteousness to a
people yet unborn,
that he has done it. (vs. 30–31)

THE FINAL TWO VERSES of our psalm need to be considered together. As the climax of the entire psalm, they encompass not only the effect of the Cross of Christ on your life and mine, but they speak to the entire world—past, present, and in the time to come.

It is not an exaggeration to say these two verses are a summary of the entire Bible and God's salvation for the world.

In order to understand these verses and their centrality to the entire biblical message, we must first suspend our notion of time, or at least attempt that feat! Consider that on the Cross, Jesus is carrying all the sins of all of history: past, present, and future. But also consider that He can "see" back into time past and forward into eternity. The Cross stands in the middle of time.

Or perhaps it would be better to call it the centerpiece *of* all time, and *for* all time.

With that in your mind and heart, consider these amazing truths from verses 30 and 31.

Verse 30 begins with a nod to the past. *"Posterity shall serve him..."* The psalm has in mind all the people who have served God in ages past. We read in the New Testament the truth of Jesus' death and resurrection, but this verse is making the bold statement that every patriarch and matriarch in the Old Testament—in their work, their lives, their faith, their witness, and their death—were in service to God *in Christ.* The gallery of the faithful mentioned in Hebrews Chapter 11 is just one example of this.

This verse also includes a look into the future. There is a sense that the witness of faithful people of the past can speak into the future. Generations yet to be born will learn of God's righteousness. Thus, the Gospel is and always will be eternal. It is truth *from* the past and truth *for* the future. And this is only possible because Jesus, on the Cross, gave His life for the past and the future. The Gospel of Jesus is like the Eternal Presence of God, the great I AM we encountered earlier.

Hope has been building through the last few verses of Psalm 22. We have felt this along our pilgrimage. And now, at the end of Jesus's amazing Psalm on the Cross, we encounter a crescendo of hope and promise that brings joy to every believer. What began in the harsh darkness of rejection, mockery, torture, is now concluding in the light of hope. Jesus spoke the first verse of Psalm 22 aloud, a headline announcement of everything that would follow. We saw this in the uncannily accurate descriptions of what was happening to our Lord, minute by minute. Then, in the second part of the psalm we see a triumphant Christ who glorifies God His Father and speaks with confidence of His final victory, even as He was dying.

We know that Jesus intended the entire text of Psalm 22 as His prayer on the Cross because here, at the end of this psalm of agony, we come face to face with eternal deliverance. Here we can see the fullness of Jesus's hope for us, for the church, and for all future generations. As Derek Kidner, has written, "No Christian can read this without being vividly confronted with the crucifixion. It is not only a matter of prophecy minutely fulfilled, but of the sufferer's humility—there is no plea for vengeance—and his vision of a world-wide ingathering of the Gentiles."[61]

Read the verses at the start of this chapter once more. *"...[T]hat he has done it!"* reveals the final truth of Psalm 22. This phrase is a near-exact echo of the final words of Jesus on the Cross. *"It is finished!"*

Can it be clearer? Jesus chose this psalm for His time on the Cross, embodying it from the first cry of dereliction to the last statement of His final accomplishment.

These final words present us with the prediction that the name and the fame of Jesus will be shared from one generation to another. It is a strong and positive message that, in an ultimate sense, the world has been set right. There is nothing more to be done. And that the focus of all future proclamations should be the Gospel—that is, the perfect work and righteousness of Jesus Christ.

CONSIDER AND COMMENT:

1. How do the last two verse of Psalm 22 summarize the entire Bible?

2. The psalm says that "posterity shall serve him." In your own words, what does this mean?

3. Looking back on Psalm 22, which verse stands out for you? Why?

—— *Finis* ——

Epilogue

THERE ARE TIMES IN THE STUDY of Holy Scripture when a diligent reader must simply pause and consider what God has provided for us in the Bible. We have been blessed with a living, Spirit-breathed document, an integrated whole that has a single focused storyline leading us to the life and death of its subject, Jesus Christ. We ought to be awed by the story of the Bible, to be sure, but we can also thank God for the Bible that conveys this life-changing story.

It has been humbling to read through this psalm with such a personal approach to the heart of Jesus. Since He is my Lord and Savior, I have tried to honor Him by offering my best and highest thoughts and meditations. If this book has been helpful to you, I am grateful for that. But I know that whatever insights I have presented will fall short of what the Holy Spirit can and will show you as you prayerfully consider our Lord and the Cross He endured.

The Apostle Paul's beautiful prayer for the church in Ephesus comes to mind as a fitting conclusion to our journey:

"For this reason I bow my knees before the Father, from whom every family in heaven and on earth is named, that according to the riches of his glory he may grant you to be strengthened with power through his Spirit in your inner being, so that Christ may dwell in your hearts through faith—that you, being rooted and grounded in love, may

have strength to comprehend with all the saints what is the breadth and length and height and depth, and to know the love of Christ that surpasses knowledge, that you may be filled with all the fullness of God.

"Now to him who is able to do far more abundantly than all that we ask or think, according to the power at work within us, to him be glory in the church and in Christ Jesus throughout all generations, forever and ever. Amen."[62]

I hope that I have approached this task with the humility to not demand this interpretation. But there is enough in the Gospels to suggest it, and I offer it to you only as a devotional suggestion.

* * * * *

We have been taking a "deep dive" into one of the most passionate psalms in the Bible. If this method helps you understand and apply the truth of God's Word in your life and you would like to do more, please keep an eye on the LeaderWorks web site. There will be other books coming in the near future that take this "deep dive" approach.

www.LeaderWorks.org

Thanks for reading!
If you enjoyed this book,
please leave an honest review
on your favorite book store platform.

Endnotes

1. The seven last words of Jesus are as follows: "Father, forgive them, for they do not know what they do" (Luke 23:34); "Truly, I say to you, today you will be with me in paradise" (Luke 23:43); "Woman, behold your son. Son, behold your mother" (John 19:26–27); "My God, My God, why have you forsaken me?" (Matthew 27:46; Mark 15:34); "I thirst" (John 19:28); "It is finished" (John 19:30); "Father, into your hands I commit my spirit" (Luke 23:46).

2. Mark 15:34; cf. Matthew 27:46.

3. Luke 2:49.

4. John 10:30. The Feast of the Dedication was a major mass gathering event in Jerusalem. It was called Hanukkah or the Festival of Lights.

5. Mark 4:35—5:43 In four different stories, Jesus demonstrates His total domination over the weather, disease, the devil, and finally even death.

6. Luke 11:1. This is where Jesus begins to teach them the Lord's Prayer.

7. I read John Stevenson's *Christ on the Cross:* In Darkness In Light. These are a series of essays or long sermons on the 22nd Psalm.

8. Deuteronomy 14:2: "For you are a holy people to YHWH your God, and God has chosen you to be his treasured people from all the nations that are on the face of the earth."

9. Howard Clark Kee, "The Function of Scriptural Quotations and Allusions in Mark 11–16," pp. 165–188 in *Jesus und Paulus: Festschrift für Werner Georg Kümmel zum 70. Geburtstag,* E.E. Earle and W.G. Kümmel, eds. (Göttingen: Vandenhoeck & Ruprecht, 1975).

10. From *The Treasury of David* by Charles H. Spurgeon regarding Psalm 103.

11. Exodus 3:14.

12. Revelation 1:8. "I am the Alpha and the Omega," says the Lord God, "who is and who was and who is to come, the Almighty."

13. John 1:1–3.

14. The "I Am" statements of Jesus in the Gospel of John are as follows: "I am the bread of life" (John 6:35, 48; see also 6:41, 51); "I am the light of the world" (8:12; 9:5); "I am the door" (10:7, 9); "I am the good shepherd" (10:11, 14); "I am the resurrection and the life" (11:25); "I am the way, and the truth, and the life" (14:6); "I am the true vine" (15:1; see also 15:5). See Jeffrey E. Miller, "I Am Sayings," ed. John D. Barry et al., *The Lexham Bible Dictionary* (Bellingham, WA: Lexham Press, 2016).

15. Isaiah 1:18.

16. From Luke 2:1ff. I will never read the Christmas story withing holding this image in my mind.

17. 1 Timothy 1:15.

18. This story is told in Luke 5.

19. Deuteronomy 3:13.

20. John 1:11.

21. Luke 4:1–13.

22. Luke 4:16–30.

23. Matthew 8:23–27.

24. Matthew 4:12–13.

25. 1 Peter 5:8.

26. C.S. Lewis, *Mere Christianity* (New York: HarperCollins, 2001), 132.

27. Mark 15:39.

28. Matthew 27:34.

29. This account is deduced from John 19:28 and Psalm 69:21.

30. Genesis 3:19.

31. Luke 22:44.

32. See Acts 2:25–35.

33. John 20:24ff.

34. John 19:23–24.

35. Matthew 8:20.

36. Job 1:21.

37. Mark 15:38–39.

38. Jeremiah 25:15.

39. Isaiah 55:8–9.

40. Matthew 26:52.

41. https://en.wikipedia.org/wiki/Notker_the_Stammerer.

42. Romans 8:18.

43. 2 Corinthians 4:17–18.

44. Revelation 21:3–4.

45. 2 Samuel 6:14.

46. Hebrews 10:25.

47. Matthew 28:10.

48. Acts 2:42ff.

49. Isaiah 6:5.

50. Genesis 32:22ff.

51. Psalm 27:8 is a prayer to God for Him not to hide His face. Sometimes it might seem as though He does, but Psalm 22 reveals the truth. He does NOT turn away.

52. James 4:8.

53. Isaiah 29:16.

54. Revelation 5:9–10.

55. Romans 7:15.

56. Matthew 6:33.

57. Mark 10:21.

58. 1 Timothy 6:10.

59. Matthew 19:24.

60. Galatians 3:28–29.

61. Derek Kidner, *Psalms 1–72*, ed. D.J. Wiseman, Tyndale Old Testament Commentaries (Downers Grove, IL: IVP, 1973), 105.

62. Ephesians 3:14–21.

DAVID H. ROSEBERRY has been an ordained Anglican minister for 40 years. He was the founding Rector of Christ Church in Plano, Texas for over 30 years. Now he is the Executive Director of Leader-Works serving churches and church leaders. *The Psalm on the Cross* is his fourth book.

ALSO BY DAVID H. ROSEBERRY
Giving Up
The Rector and the Vestry
When the Lord is My Shepherd
The Ordinary Ways of God (Spring 2021)
Come Before Winter (Summer 2021)

Made in the USA
Coppell, TX
31 January 2021